88-16457

808.02
EVE

53612

Everhart, Nancy
So you have to write
a term paper!

808.02   88-16457
EVE

Everhart, N$_a$ncy

So you have to write a term
paper

53612

K

SO YOU HAVE TO
WRITE A TERM PAPER!

NANCY EVERHART

SO YOU HAVE TO WRITE A TERM PAPER!

FRANKLIN WATTS I 1987
NEW YORK I LONDON I TORONTO I SYDNEY
A LANGUAGE POWER BOOK

Cartoons by Anne Canevari Green

Photographs courtesy of:
Henry Rasof: pp. 27, 28, 76, 77;
Salvatore Tocci: pp. 36, 37, 40;
CLSI, Inc.: pp. 44, 45.

Library of Congress Cataloging-in-Publication Data

Everhart, Nancy.
So you have to write a term paper!

(A Language power book)
Bibliography: p.
Includes index.
Summary: Describes the steps in writing a term
paper, including choosing a topic, doing research,
writing an outline, taking notes, doing a rough draft,
and editing the final paper.
1. Report writing. 2. Research. [1. Report writing.
2. Research] I. Title. II. Series.
LB1047.3.E94 1987   808'.02   87-8251
ISBN 0-531-10427-3

88-16457

53612

ACKNOWLEDGMENTS

I would like to thank the following people for the role they played in making this book possible: my husband, Harry Everhart, for his encouragement and support; my editor, Henry Rasof, for his patience and insight; Doris Epler and Dick Cassel of the Pennsylvania Department of Education, School Libraries Division, for their foresight in educating Pennsylvania school librarians in technology; Donna Toler-Baumbach and Gary Orwig of the University of Central Florida, for my first training on computers; James Fogarty and Jean Tuzinski, my two good friends and pioneers in the library/computing field; Joseph Rudawski, for his support of my computerized library; and Matt Gimmer, Sam Schaeffer, and Maria Jacketti, for use of their term papers.

CONTENTS

SO YOU HAVE TO
WRITE A TERM PAPER!

TO THE READER

1

The inevitable has happened: you have been assigned a term paper. If you are like many students, your palms may start to sweat, your heart may race, your throat may constrict. You are, plain and simple, scared. Even if you aren't scared, admit it: you feel just a little nervous. You also may feel annoyed about all that time you will be spending on an assignment you didn't ask for.

When the assignment was given, probably your whole class groaned. Take heart, then: you're not alone in your fears, or minor anxiety, or annoyance. In fact, since all students have to write term papers at one time or another, whether they are in elementary school or college, you've got a lot of company. They number in the millions.

This book tells you what a term paper is and shows you how to write a good one. Information on using a computer in your task is included, because there's a good chance you have access to one.

Using a computer will make your job easier, but you can still write a perfectly decent paper without one: lots of term papers were written before the introduction of computers, and lots more are bound to be. At the same time, using a computer won't guarantee you an A.

Reading *So You Have to Write a Term Paper!* will provide you with the knowledge you need to overcome the fears—or minor anxiety—you might have in dealing with the inevitable assignment of a term paper. It will also help you to turn a required assignment into one you meet head-on in anticipation of pleasure, not boredom or drudgery.

A FEW LITTLE HINTS

Two things can make your job monumentally easier:

1. Start the assignment early rather than waiting until the week before the paper is due. Divide your time into three blocks: (*a*) choosing the topic, (*b*) doing research, and (*c*) writing. The first section is the shortest; the last two will probably be equally long.
2. Ask your teacher questions, either in class or in private, about anything you aren't clear about, from the color of the paper you have to type on to the fine points of the topic.

WHAT IS A TERM PAPER?
WHY WRITE ONE?

2

A term paper is usually assigned to encourage you to learn more about a subject and to test various skills you may have learned in a class. Your teacher may want to see what you have learned or can learn about a subject, or to see if you can think critically, do research, or write effectively—or all of these.

Term papers are often assigned at the beginning of a class. Sometimes they count for a major share of your grade. If you go to college, you will find out that in some classes the term paper may be the only graded assignment you receive. In fact, your final grade may be based entirely on your grade on the paper and on the final exam.

Doing a good job on your term paper will not only help you get a good grade in your classes now, but will help you do well in college. Of course, there is more to life than grades. That's why it's important to work in such a way that you are actually interested in what you are doing. If you have a choice of topics, this means choosing an interesting topic—interesting to you.

ORIGINALITY

Few teachers expect papers of earthshaking originality, but they do want something that exhibits some evidence of original thinking. They want you to use your brain. Many students simply rehash subjects already adequately covered in encyclopedia articles.

The nature of your term paper will of course depend on any special instructions from your teacher. There are three main types of term papers:

The first kind consists of your ideas about something or somebody, for example, your criticism of a new novel by Judy Blume, or your interpretation of a short story by Ernest Hemingway.

The second kind is a new interpretation of a body of knowledge, for example, your theory that the dinosaurs were not wiped out by a meteorite but instead by a volcanic eruption.

The third kind consists of a bulk of information assembled in a new way, for example, a comparison of the plots in silent films with those in talkies.

Each of these topics reflects some original thinking.

Of course, anyone can offer an opinion or interpretation, or can organize facts. What distinguishes a term paper from an essay is the body of facts you provide to support your views; you aren't just going to spout off your opinions. Similarly, your comparison is not just going to be two lists; you are going to interpret the similarities and differences.

A term paper has to involve research. Your topic has to lend itself to detective work to uncover the information you need to criticize, interpret, or assemble and compare. Although most research for term papers is done in libraries, research also can be done through interviews, experimentation, and surveys. Sometimes, in fact, the best way to learn about a new field (like cryptozoology) is to talk to an expert. Still, most of your research will involve information gathered from printed matter and, in some cases, from computers, video-discs, filmstrips, videotapes, and other media.

Your term paper is probably not going to win you a Pulitzer Prize or a Nobel Prize, although it might be the first step in a career leading to one. But you will learn how to think and how to work with information, extremely important talents in an age in which everyone is deluged with information about everything from auto-mobiles to zebras.

Now that you have a slightly better idea of the nature of a term paper, you may feel a little less anxious about your assignment and a little more excited about learning how to choose and work with term-paper topics.

TOPICS FOR TERM PAPERS

3

Topics for term papers are either assigned or left up to you to choose—or some combination.

If you are assigned a very specific topic and have no choice whatsoever in the matter, you might want to move on to the next chapter.

CHOOSE A TOPIC
THAT INTERESTS YOU

You will do a better job on your paper—and have more fun—if you choose a topic that interests you, that *really* interests you.

Many assigned topics are very general. Your history teacher may want you to do research on the Old West. You will have to decide exactly what to write on. Or your science teacher may be covering a unit on whales. You are to write on some aspect of whales, but the ultimate choice of *what* to write is yours.

These assignments give you less leeway than the assignment to just "write a term paper on history." But if you use your imagination and don't get bogged down in thinking, "Oh, the Civil War is boring" or "I don't know what to say about whales," you will be ahead of a good many of your classmates.

A good way to approach either type of assignment—restricted or unlimited—is to try to relate the topic to a hobby or to simply write about one of your hobbies.

A car nut could turn a report on the Soviet Union into a comparison of styles of American and Soviet automobiles. A drawing enthusiast could write on famous black artists for a paper on black Americans. A more substantial topic might be an investigation of the role of black artists in the art world, or an attempt to answer the question, "Is there such a thing as a 'black style' in America?"

Other possible tie-ins:

- A chemistry report could focus on the cosmetic industry if you enjoy experimenting with make-up.
- An English paper could probe into a writer's background to find out if a tragic love affair affected his or her poetry—if you are an incurable romantic.

Make sure that if you choose something based on one of your hobbies or pet interests, the subject is worth writing about and can be researched. "Sun signs in your life" could be frivolous, as could "Why MTV is the best TV station." These topics are not suitable for research papers because neither requires any research to write on.

Don't make the mistake of thinking that only things taught in school are worth writing about. Astronomy may not be taught in your school, but it's a subject that lends itself to a lot of possibilities.

You may need to do some preliminary reading to help you choose your topic—to learn more about a subject, to see if the subject really interests you, to see how much has been published on the subject, and to see if it really is suitable for a term paper. Write down the titles and authors of any sources you consult.

REFINE YOUR TOPIC

Some Topics Are Too Broad

Chances are that your teacher's general topic or your own initial choice of topics will have to be narrowed down, or refined. "Whales" is too broad, as are "The Old West" and "Hispanic History," "Black Americans," "Chemistry," and "Cars."

Why bother narrowing your topic? Although these sound like perfectly respectable subjects, using them as they are will quickly get you in trouble.

- There is no way you can do a good job writing on whales in general in, say a ten-page paper, or even a twenty-page one. There is too much to say about whales, and you will end up with a superficial paper. At the very least, you would need to write an entire book to do justice to the subject!
- It's hard to do anything original with a vague topic like "The Old West" or "Whales" or "Chemistry." All you will have is a vast collection of facts.
- Tackling a subject like "Whales" instead of one like "The Feeding Habits of the Blue Whale in the South Pacific" will require you to sift through too many references. Whereas you might have to read a hundred books and five hundred articles on whales in general, you might have to

read only a few books and maybe a dozen articles on the feeding habits of one particular species of whale in one part of a very large ocean.

- Organizing all the information you attempt to gather from these hundreds of sources will be such an overwhelming task that you probably will never get around to writing the paper!

Most readers would rather learn a lot about a narrow topic than a little about a broad topic. They will have a hard time grasping the same facts you had a hard time presenting.

Some Topics Are Too Narrow
A topic can also be too narrow.

What is wrong with that? After all, less work is required.

- A topic that is too limited will end up being overly specialized. Readers may be interested in the feeding habits of the blue whale, but unless they are marine biologists, they probably won't be interested in an exhaustive study of the migration habits of the blue whale's main food supply. However, if you are writing a research paper for a biology class, such a topic may be just what is required.
- If your topic is too narrow, you may be unable to find enough information—the opposite problem of too much information. No books may exist on some extremely rarefied topics, and the only articles may be very specialized. These articles may be hard to understand, and just as your readers may be bored by the migration patterns of krill, so might you.

Making Choices

How do you tell whether a topic is too narrow or too broad? For one thing, topics that are too broad sound that way:

History
Advertising
Biology
Sports
Travel
The Occult
Immigrants

These are, in some cases, entire disciplines. When you look up these topics in the card catalog at the library or in the *Reader's Guide to Periodical Literature,* you also may find too many sources (like a thousand articles on history, two hundred books on sports, eighty books on astrology alone!). Narrowing these topics down:

The Civil War
Television Advertising
Trees
Baseball
Travel in China
Astrology
Asian-American Immigrants
    in the United States

Still too vague: you already have found eighty books on astrology, and you noticed tons of articles on baseball when you did your first search in the library. The Civil War may present a problem, too: How can you possibly describe the entire Civil War in ten pages, or twenty pages, or even a hundred? Going a step further:

The Effect of the Civil War on Families Living in the North and South

Does Television Advertising of Beer Lead to Increased Alcoholism?

The Effects of Acid Rain on Redwoods in Oregon

Comparison of the Pitching of Dwight Gooden and Sandy Koufax

The Effects of Foreign Travel in China on Restaurants in China

The Role of Astrology in Hollywood High Society

Comparison of Quality of Life of Vietnamese Immigrants in Texas Before and After the Vietnam War

We now *seem* to have more manageable topics.

Visit the library again and find out if too much information is available—or not enough. This involves checking the card catalog, major periodical indexes, and maybe an on-line data base to get a rough idea of the quantity and types of sources that exist on your topic. You may be interested in knowing that an on-line service such as Bibliographic Retrieval System (BRS) might list hundreds or even thousands of articles on some topics.

Wait a minute. You have chosen the last topic, on Vietnamese immigrants, and find absolutely nothing on immigration before the Vietnam War. Your topic is *too narrow*.

If this initial library work turns up too many or too few sources on your narrowed-down topic, you will have to return to the drawing board to either refine or broaden the topic. Chapters 5 and 6 tell you more about the many different sources you will need for your research.

BRAINSTORM

The process of choosing or refining a topic can involve *brainstorming*—letting your imagination run wild and writing down any topic that pops into your head, or "creatively" refining. From a list of brainstormed topics you can eliminate those topics that seem farfetched or are too broad or too narrow. Creative refining can lead to a brilliant approach to your topic.

Here are two examples.

1. You are assigned a research paper, but the choice of topic is all yours.

    You sit down, pen in hand, close your eyes, let your mind wander, and start jotting down all the ideas that come to mind, without thinking whether they are too broad, too narrow, or even appropriate for school: calligraphy, writing, models, model ships, sailing, vacations, cruises in the Caribbean, famous pirates, South America, Cortez, drugs in Colombia, jungles, cocaine, smuggling, police brutality, karate, wrestling, Cyndi Lauper, television . . .

2. You are assigned a general topic like "Science." You might focus your brainstorming:

    The life of a certain scientist
    Defending or disproving a scientific theory
    Describing in detail a plant, animal, element, planet
    Explaining how a certain scientific discovery has affected our lives
    Determining what the future may bring because of certain discoveries

Although too broad, perhaps, or impractical, you at least have a place to begin. This technique is especially useful if you haven't the slightest idea what you want to write on.

"HELP! I STILL CAN'T THINK OF A TOPIC"

If you are stuck and can't think of *anything* to write about, don't give up. The world is a big place, you're smarter than you think, and school isn't *that* boring. There's got to be something for you to write about.

Go to your teacher. That's right. Get up the courage to talk to your teacher about your problem. Probably your teacher will either suggest a bunch of topics or will gently try to get you to think of a topic on your own. Your teacher may ask you about your interests and subtly lead you to your very own idea.

You also can look through collections of topics written especially for people in your shoes. One such book is *10,000 Ideas for Term Papers, Projects and Reports,* written by Kathryn Lamm and published by Arco (New York, 1984).

Another good source of ideas is the index volume of an encyclopedia. One encyclopedia includes the following entries under the heading "Greece, Ancient":

How Alexander spread Greek culture
Citizenship in ancient Greece
Funeral customs
Medicine
Advances in science
The Trojan War

Check other reference sources, too. The *New York Times* index is a good one for news items; the *Scientific American* annual index may give you ideas for science reports. Thumb through current issues of your favorite magazines or of magazines related to your assigned topic, if you have one.

Another approach is to use a computer program such as the *Americana Topic Finder and Research Planner.* This software takes broad topics you are

You can explore the following areas:

1 Literature
2 History and Social Studies
3 Science, Technology, and
  the Unexplained
4 Art
5 Music and Dance
6 Sports and Literature

0 None of these

Type the number of your choice.

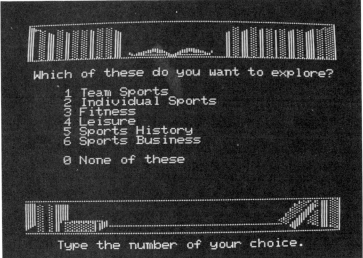

Which of these do you want to explore?

1 Team Sports
2 Individual Sports
3 Fitness
4 Leisure
5 Sports History
6 Sports Business

0 None of these

Type the number of your choice.

The American Topic Finder and Research Planner *is designed to help students choose term paper topics. A succession of menus, two of which are shown here and two on the next page, lead you to various topics and to encyclopedia articles on the topics.*

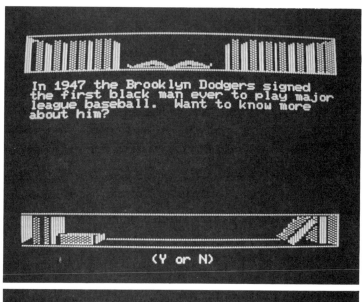

In 1947 the Brooklyn Dodgers signed the first black man ever to play major league baseball. Want to know more about him?

(Y or N)

In volume 23 you'll read about Jackie Robinson's brilliant career as a college athlete, as an Army officer during World War II, and as a professional baseball player.

When you have read that, come back to find some more interesting topics.

Press SPACE BAR.

Two additional menus from the Americana Topic Finder and Research Planner assigned, questions you about your own interests, and then provides a list of possible term-paper topics. This particular program even goes on to list reference materials that contain the information you need.

And last but not least, talk to your school or public librarian. He or she has a lot of experience helping people with research papers—people just like you.

THE PRELIMINARY OUTLINE

4

Once you feel secure and happy with your topic, write down a one-paragraph statement of it. For instance, if your topic is "The Development of a Black Point of View in Art," your paragraph might be:

> *This paper will develop the idea that black artists have a special point of view related to being black. Six artists will be studied. Their descriptions of their art will be combined with my descriptions of their art. I will show that each of these artists has been influenced most strongly by upbringing, racial issues, color barriers, and "black consciousness."*

You then need to flesh out this summary in anticipation of a serious attack on the library. A good way to do this is to construct a preliminary—or planning—outline. This needn't be a formal outline of the kind you have probably been learning how to write since the fourth grade. All you have to do is jot down some ideas on your topic in some kind of order.

A good way to do this is to sit in a quiet place by yourself with a pad of paper and a pencil or pen and close your eyes. (You should be an old pro at this by now.) Bring your topic before your eyes: "Wyatt Earp," "Blue Whales," "Black Women Artists," "Soviet Ballet Dancers," "Irony in the Writing of Irving Wallace"—whatever.

Mull over the topic. Stretch it out. Look at one aspect of it. Visualize the car, or the art, or the whale. Develop thoughts about aspects of your topic and follow these thoughts along main and side roads. What's most interesting about Wyatt Earp? His shooting ability? His behavior with women? His strong friendships?

How do the Russians manage to train such wonderful dancers when they build such lousy refrigerators? Maybe it's something in the national spirit. Yes, even in the nineteenth century they could do some things well and other things just terribly.

You are developing your paper by "writing it in your head," before you even know much about the subject. Because you have done little reading, you will be unable to do too much of this, but you can do enough to help you settle at least on an approach to the topic.

As you turn up interesting thoughts, questions, conclusions, and avenues of discussion, jot them down. Let your mind wander over the topic in the same way it did when you were brainstorming on the topic. Soon you will have several pages covered with notes. You can then sort through these notes, put them on index cards, or simply print them neatly on a fresh sheet of paper (or punch them into your computer), and set aside the material you have weeded out. Arrange the organized notes and questions in the order you think you'll want to approach them in your paper.

The Secret of Soviet Ballet — A Few Notes

History — always great

Origins?

Early teachers and stars and their influence

How, even during the Stalinist period, was ballet supported and kept traditional (?)

Competition with West

Defectors — Nureyev, Makarova, Baryshnikov

Comparison of present and past dancers

Rough notes on your topic can later be turned into a more formal outline.

If you are unable to work in this fashion, you can simply do your thinking on paper: bypass the closed-eyes stage and just jot down your ideas. Then select and organize them as before.

Whichever way you work, also make notes on possible illustrations.

You are now ready to learn about the different reference materials you will be using to help you prepare your preliminary bibliography.

REFERENCE SOURCES

5

So much information is available today that many people call the time we live in the Information Age. The key to learning about one specific subject—without drowning in information—is to use reference sources.

Reference sources such as the card catalog, encyclopedias, special books, and interviews provide concise information on your subject that is invaluable when you are doing preliminary reading. They also provide the names of the more specific sources you will need when compiling your bibliography.

Where will you find the books, articles, pamphlets, maps, directories, cassettes, photographs, dictionaries, videotapes, and microflim you need for your term paper? In the most important reference source of all: the library.

THE LIBRARY

Libraries tend to be laid out in different ways, but their materials are organized in pretty much the same way.

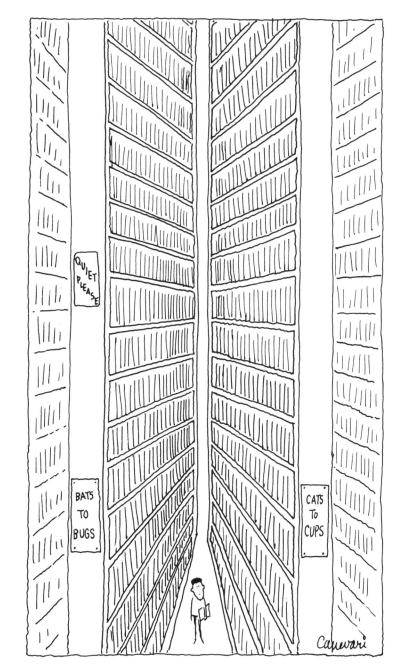

*Reference shelves, document drawers,
special reference materials, microfilm machines,
and microfiche readers*

Reference materials such as encyclopedias, almanacs, the *Who's Who*, various directories, and "short histories" are usually found in one place. In a large library, this place will be large—occupying many shelves and rows. In a small library, these materials may be found in a few stacks of shelves. Reference books can sometimes be checked out for twenty-four hours in a school library, but usually must be used in the library. Such materials usually contain an *R* in front of the call letter—*R* for Reference.

A card catalog will contain special cards telling you which books are contained in this particular library. Many libraries now have computerized "card" catalogs, and some (for example, the New York Public Library) have put the card catalog information in book form. Reference books are also listed in the card catalog. Bound periodicals are listed either in the catalog or on separate lists.

There will be a *Readers' Guide to Periodical Literature* and perhaps an index to the *New York Times* (whose motto is "All the news that's fit to print"). These may be located near the card file or book catalogs.

Fiction is organized on the shelves by the last name of the author, not by call number. Nonfiction is organized by a call number. There are two systems—Library of Congress and Dewey Decimal. Each has a different way for organizing nonfiction.

Current magazines are usually found on a rack, back issues on shelves, either loose or bound. The same goes for newspapers, although back issues of the *New York Times* will be found on microfilm. Your library probably has a couple of microfilm readers.

Documents such as government publications are usually found on shelves or in drawers. The microfilm readers and computers may have their own section.

Since knowing your way around the library will save you a great deal of time, either ask your teacher to take your class on a library tour or have your librarian show you around. Some libraries may have brochures describing their layout, holdings, and use. A small library is easy to get to know, but a large library may be intimidating at first. Once you know where to look, you will be speeding around as if you own the place!

Now that you know where to locate the materials in your library, you will benefit from learning how to use them.

THE CARD CATALOG

The card catalog is often called the "key to the library," and for good reason. It is an index to nearly all of the materials to be found in that library.

The card catalog also tells you where a source is located. It does this by providing a call number for each book or periodical. The library in turn is organized by groups of materials having similar call numbers. Each catalog card gives the call number (either numbers or letters or a combination) in the upper left-hand corner. Once you match that number with the number of the book or periodical on the shelf, you are on your way.

Most card catalogs are centrally located in the library, although in large libraries you may find card catalogs in several locations.

Card catalogs usually consist of a cabinet or cabinets with several (or many, depending on the size of the library) drawers. The drawers are alphabetized, as are the cards inside the drawers. Many libraries have on-line catalogs, which are accessed using a computer terminal. Some libraries have book-type card catalogs.

Information is accessed from the card catalog (and other catalogs) by subject, by author, and by title. Some libraries have a totally separate catalog for each of these categories.

Although the card catalog lists more than books, most people tend to use the card catalog to locate books.

The card catalog is the key to the library.

Let's look at a few examples of how to obtain information on a topic.

You have either decided to write on Iceland and are looking for a way to narrow your subject, or you have your final topic and are preparing your bibliography.

You look in the card catalog under Iceland and find nothing listed. Don't give up yet. It is possible that you are looking in the wrong place. Because the card catalog follows the word-by-word method of alphabetizing instead of the letter-by-letter method used in dictionaries, Iceland will come after Ice Skating. Be careful you don't get thrown when you are looking up compound words.

It also is possible that your library has no books on Iceland. But wait. Although no one book may be dedicated to the country of Iceland, information on Iceland might be in other sources.

Iceland is part of Europe. Check the card catalog under Europe, find those books, and look in the index. No doubt you will find information on Iceland.

Similarly, if you can't find a whole book on the *Titanic*, look under Ships or Disasters. Pygmies will be covered in books about Africa or Blacks—History. Books on alcoholism may be filed under Alcohol or Drug Abuse. Information on Wyatt Earp can probably be found in books about the Old West.

Try to think of the broader picture and where your topic fits in. Here are some more examples:

Not Listed:	Check:
trout	fishes/fishing
oranges	fruit
Declaration of Independence	U.S. History/Revolution
Buckingham Palace	England/Great Britain
Globe Theatre	Shakespeare

Not Listed:	Check:
Oracles	Religion
Van Halen	Music—Rock
Lee Iacocca	Biography/Encyclopedia

Often the cards in the catalog themselves will direct you to alternative subjects. These cards are called "see references" or "see also references" or "cross references." When you look up Alcoholism, a card may say, "See Alcohol." Sifting through several cards on alcoholism may lead you to a card that says "See Also Alcohol."

You also may want to search for a specific author. Perhaps you already know that Bruce Catton is a famous writer about the Civil War. You can look up "Catton, Bruce" in the card catalog to see if his books are in your library. Always look up names—whether they are names of authors or names of subjects—by the last name, first.

The last way to look up information is by title. Reference books can be looked up this way. (You may want to see which ones your library has before you actually head for the shelves.) If you are looking for a specific book—*The Sea Around Us*—you would do it by title. Disregard articles—A, An, and The—when they are the first word of a title, because so have the cataloguers. To find *The Sea Around Us*, look in the *S* drawer or under *S*. The *Encyclopedia of Mammals* will be listed under *E*, not under *T*.

Catalog cards can give you a lot more information than the call number, subject, name of the author, and title. You can, for example, tell what the book is about, whether it contains photographs or ilustrations, how long it is, and when it was published.

This information can be invaluable. If you are doing a report on computers and find a book published over five years ago, you may want to disregard it. Probably there will be little or nothing mentioned about personal computers. If illustrations are a central part of your paper, you can distinguish the books with lots of illustrations from those with very few. The short summary on the catalog card will give you a feeling for the contents of the book.

You also can obtain most of the information you need for your bibliography directly from the card catalog.

On-line catalogs work on much the same principle as regular card catalogs. However, instead of flipping through cards, you type in either the subject, name of the author, or title on a keyboard, and the computer searches for the relevant references for you. The information then comes up on the screen. You can either write down what you need on paper or, if the terminal is connected to a printer, print it out.

An on-line system has many advantages over the traditional card catalog:

- The computer knows how the information is alphabetized.
- The computer makes no distinction among requests for titles, authors, or subjects. Were you to type in "Albert Einstein," for example, you would get books by him and about him as well as books entitled Albert Einstein.
- Reponse time is quick.
- You may be able to find out if a book has been checked out.
- You may be able to access the information from home, if you have the equipment.
- You may be able to access the holdings of other libraries as well as you own.
- The computer automatically checks all the "see" and "see also" cards for you.

```
                    CLSI Welcomes You
                   To a Demonstration of
                          CL-CAT
       The Next Generation Online Public Access Catalog

       You May Search the Catalog Using Any of the Methods
       Listed Below.  Choose By Pressing the Corresponding
       Number Key.  You may Request Assistance at Any Time
       By Pressing the HELP Key.

       TO SEARCH BY:  (1)  SUBJECT

                      (2)  AUTHOR

                      (3)  TITLE

                      (4)  AUTHOR AND TITLE

                      (5)  ALL CATEGORIES

                      (6)  CALL NUMBER

       PRESS SELECTION NUMBER, OR PRESS  (7)
       FOR OTHER DATABASES _
```

```
                        SUBJECT SEARCH




       TYPE SUBJECT WORD(S)

       SUBJECT=MUSIC AND EDUCATION_


       PRESS
            BROWSE To See Alphabetic Listing of Subjects.
            KEYWORD To Find Your Word(s) as Part of a Subject.




       Press HELP for an Explanation of BROWSE and KEYWORD .


       HELP for Assistance.              START OVER Completely.
```

*Using an on-line card catalog may help you
in your search for reference sources.*

SEARCH HISTORY

NO. SEARCH TERMS   REFERENCES FOUND
----
1.   SUBJECT=MUSIC AND EDUCATION   10

Press Line Number for Brief References.
Or PRESS: _

COMPOSE a Search.
HELP for Assistance.   START OVER Completely.

BRIEF REFERENCES

SEARCH TERM(S): SUBJECT=MUSIC AND EDUCATION
REFERENCES FOUND: 10   Page 1 of 2
NO.   AUTHOR   TITLE   DATE FORMAT
--- -------------------- -------------------------- ---- ------
1.   Music for the exceptional child /   1975 BOOK
2.   Music in developmental therapy :a curri 1976 BOOK
3.   Physical and creative activities for th 1979 BOOK
4.   Rhythm & pulse   1967 AV
5. Anshel, Mark H   The effect of music and rhythm on the a 1978 BOOK
6. Beattie, James,Bea   Essays:on poetry and music, as they aff 1779 BOOK
7. Beattie, James,Bea   Essays.On the nature and immutability o 1776 BOOK
8. Cramer, Mary Valen   The effect of musical stimuli during mo 1974 MICRFM
9. Dickinson, Pamela   Music with ESN children :a guide for th 1976 BOOK

Press Line Number to Select Your Choice: _

Or PRESS:
NEXT Page.   SEARCH HISTORY to Enter Next Search.

HELP for Assistance.   START OVER Completely.

ENCYCLOPEDIAS

To many students, doing research means going to an encyclopedia and copying information from articles word for word. This is plagiarism—literary theft—and is totally unacceptable.

Other students, aware of the pitfalls of copying, mistakenly view the articles in encyclopedias as the last word on their topic and use no other resources. This, too, is unacceptable, although it is not plagiarism.

Encyclopedias are useful for giving you an overview of your topic and helping you find its major points and highlights. They are also useful for looking up facts. The encyclopedia is a good starting point for your research, but it definitely should not be the only source you use. (Indeed, you really don't need to consult an encyclopedia. You may want to, but you don't have to.)

The best way to extract the information from an encyclopedia is to go to the index. If you are researching falcons, for example, you will find information on these birds in volumes other than the "F" one. Only by looking in the index would you know this.

Your library should have one or more of the following major encyclopedias:

Academic American Encyclopedia
Collier's Encyclopedia
Compton's Encyclopedia and Fact-Index
Encyclopedia Americana
Merit Student's Encyclopedia
The New Book of Knowledge
The New Encyclopedia Britannica
The New Standard Encyclopedia
The World Book Encyclopedia

Encyclopedias are now becoming available on-line and on laser disk. Going on-line means connecting your computer to a another computer over telephone lines. On-line encyclopedias can be used if you have a device called a modem that enables your computer to "talk" to the computers at information services, called data banks, over the telephone. Some of the more popular services are BRS (Bibliographic Retrieval System), DIALOG, and CompuServe. Data banks store large amounts of information (called data bases) in central computers.

Laser-disk encyclopedias contain all the information that you would find in a set of encyclopedias, on a compact five-inch disk like the ones used for playing music. A special player is needed to hook up laser disks to a personal computer. This new technology is expected to grow tremendously in the near future.

With on-line and laser-disk encyclopedias, you simply type in key words dealing with your topic and get back a list of relevant articles. You can then view the articles on a monitor or print them out. There is no need to look in several volumes for material on falcons, since the computer does it for you. On-line encyclopedias are very up-to-date since new information can be added more often than it can in hardcover books.

Software is available if you need tutoring to help you use encyclopedias.

SUBJECT REFERENCE BOOKS

Before reading articles in periodicals or attacking the card catalog in search of specific books on your subject, you may want to look in reference books devoted just to your topic.

Each subject area has its special information sources. These books are useful and authoritative but like encyclopedias should be viewed as starting points. Some provide overviews; others have excellent bibliographies. Many others are really only useful for finding and checking specialized facts.

OTHER GENERAL
REFERENCE SOURCES

Almanacs contain a wide variety of information—especially statistics—updated yearly. These facts can be used to back up statements in your report. You can find out who won the Academy Award for best actor in 1954, the results of presidential elections, the circulation of magazines, the addresses of associations and so forth.

The *Statistical Abstract of the United States* is a handy tool. Most libraries keep it in the reference section. This book contains almost every kind of statistic imaginable, from the number of telephones in the United States to the number of people holding doctoral degrees. Such statistics can make your paper more interesting and authoritative. You may even be able to base your entire paper on statistics. You could use statistics about immigration, for example, as the starting point of an analysis of U.S. immigration laws.

Government documents are also useful. Libraries often store these in what is called the vertical file. Sometimes these documents are indexed in the card catalog; sometimes they are not. If they are not, just look up the topic in the vertical file, which will be organized alphabetically.

Organizations such as the American Heart Association and the Dairy Council publish pamphlets. In fact, you can pretty much assume that whatever people do or think is bound to have led someone to start an organization to disseminate information on what these people do and think, whether it's building space ships or building rubber frogs, whether it's fighting crime or fighting cockroaches. Every industry has a trade organization; every cause has organized advocates. Your parents probably receive a lot of junk mail from these organizations asking for money. (You could even do a research paper on this phenomenon of American society!)

NAMES OF SOURCES

Here are some of the standard reference books.

ANIMALS AND PLANTS

Biology Data Book
Common Insects of North America
Dictionary of Zoology
The Encyclopedia of Mammals
Gray's Manual of Botany
Grzimek's Animal Life Encyclopedia
Larousse Encyclopedia of Animal Life
Nature Atlas of America
Oxford Book of Wild Flowers
Oxford Companion to Animal Behavior
Plants of the World
Science Dictionary of the Animal World
Simon and Schuster's Guide to Trees
Wild Flowers of the United States
The World of Birds

EARTH AND SPACE

*A Brief Guide to Sources of Scientific and Technical
    Information*
Cambridge Encyclopedia of Astronomy
Evironment USA
Field Guide to Rocks and Minerals
Grzimek's Encyclopedia of Ecology
The Living Earth
McGraw-Hill Encyclopedia of Science and Technology
McGraw-Hill Yearbook of Science and Technology
Rand McNally Atlas of the Solar System
US Energy Atlas
US Geological Survey

ECONOMICS

Commodity Yearbook
Dictionary of Insurance

Economic Atlas of the United States
The Economics Reference Book
Encyclopedia of Advertising
Encyclopedia of Banking and Finance
Handbook of Labor Statistics
Handbook of Modern Accounting
International Almanac of Business and Finance
The Labor Reference Book
Marketing Handbook
McGraw-Hill Dictionary of Modern Economics
New York Times Guide to Business and Finance
Oxford Economic Atlas of the World
Profile of the United States Economy

EVENTS/HISTORY

American Book of Days
Dictionary of American History
Dictionary of the Middle Ages
Encyclopedia of American Foreign Policy
Encyclopedia of Military History
Encyclopedia of World History
European Political Facts 1789–1918
Facts on File
Harper Encyclopedia of the Modern World
Harvard Guide to American History
Historical Tables: 58 B.C.–A.D. 1978
This Fabulous Century
Times Atlas of the World
Times Atlas of World History
The Twentieth Century
UN Statistical Yearbook
US Bureau of the Census: Statistical Abstract of the
    United States

THE HUMANITIES

Bibliography of American Literature

■ 50

*Bibliography of North American Folklore and
   Folksong*
Columbia Dictionary of Modern European Literature
Contemporary Literary Criticism
Crowell's Handbook of Classical Literature
Dictionary of Classical Mythology
Dictionary of Mythology, Folklore and Symbols
Encyclopedia of World Art
Focal Encyclopedia of Photography
Granger's Index to Poetry
Harvard Dictionary of Music
History of Costume
International Cyclopedia of Music and Musicians
Literary History of the United States
McGraw-Hill Encyclopedia of World Drama
New Cambridge Bibliography of English Literature
New Grove Dictionary of Music and Musicians
New Oxford History of Music
New York Times Directory of the Film
Oxford Companion to American Literature
Oxford Companion to Art
Oxford Companion to Classical Literature
Oxford Companion to English Literature
Oxford Companion to Film
Penguin Dictionary of Architecture
Theatre World
Visual Dictionary of Art

IDEAS AND ISSUES

Dictionary of Marxist Thought
Dictionary of Philosophy and Psychology
Dictionary of the History of Ideas
Encyclopedia Judaica
Encyclopedia of Psychology
Encyclopedia of Religion and Ethics
Great Contemporary Issues

History of Philosophy
International Encyclopedia of the Social Sciences
New Century Classical Handbook
New Encyclopedia of Philosophy
New Catholic Encyclopedia

MACHINES, INVENTIONS, TECHNOLOGY

Encyclopedia of Computer Science
Encyclopedia of Computers and Data Processing
Encyclopedia of Electronics
Eureka! An Illustrated History of Inventions from the
    Wheel to the Computer
History of Technology
Technology
The Way Things Work: An Encyclopedia of Modern
    Technology

PEOPLE/BIOGRAPHY

Current Biography
Dictionary of American Biography
Dictionary of International Biography
Dictionary of National Biography
Dictionary of Scientific Biography
Encyclopedia of Black America
Index to Scientists of the World
Index to Women of the World from Ancient to Modern
    Times
International Who's Who
McGraw-Hill Encyclopedia of World Biography
McGraw-Hill Modern Men of Science
New Grove Dictionary of Music and Musicians
New York Times Obituaries Index
Notable American Women
Webster's American Biographies
Webster's Biographical Dictionary
Who's Who Among Black Americans
Who's Who in America

Who's Who in American Art
Who Was Who in America
World Who's Who in Science

Encyclopedia of the Third World
Europa Yearbook
National Geographic Atlas of the World
Rand McNally Collegiate World Atlas
The Times Atlas of the World
World Almanac and Book of Facts
World Facts and Figures
Worldmark Encyclopedia of the Nations

CRC Handbook of Chemistry and Physics
Concise Chemical and Technical Dictionary
Dictionary of Biology
Encyclopedia of Chemical Technology
Encyclopedia of Chemistry
McGraw-Hill Encyclopedia of Science and Technology
Physician's Desk Reference
Stedman's Medical Dictionary

PERIODICALS AND PERIODICAL INDEXES

Periodical is just another name for magazine. They are called periodicals because they come out periodically—weekly, monthly, or at other intervals. Periodicals are useful or often essential for a variety of reasons:

- The information they contain is more current than that found in books or encyclopedias.
- They cover topics too new to have been covered in books.

- They cover familiar topics in new ways.
- They are a good source of pictures. BUT: DO NOT CUT UP PERIODICALS FOR THE PICTURES. MAKE PHOTOCOPIES.

How do you locate information in periodicals? Let's suppose your report is on herbal medicine. In which periodical would you look? Would you consult the card catalog? Would you start paging through all the magazines in the library until you came up with some on herbal medicine?

You wouldn't consult the card catalog, since articles are not indexed there. And looking through all the magazines in your library would take a long time. Even a small library subscribes to several dozen magazines and probably has back issues of other magazines as well. A large library may contain hundreds of different periodicals. You may be interested to know that thousands of periodicals of every imaginable kind are published in the United States—thousands more if you count foreign magazines as well.

Your job is made easy by indexes to the articles published in these periodicals. And the index to begin with for almost all except the most specialized topics is the *Readers' Guide to Periodical Literature*—called the *Readers' Guide* for short.

The *Readers' Guide* takes some of the most popular magazines and lists the subjects covered in alphabetical order. It also indexes articles by author. However, 95 percent of the time you look something up, it will be by subject. The *Readers' Guide* does not index articles by title.

The *Guide* is published twice a month in September, October, December, March, April, and June and monthly in January, February, May, July, August, and November. There are also quarterly and yearly compilations. The first few pages in the *Guide* list the magazines indexed and tell you all the abbreviations used.

To find listings for herbal medicine, you would look under Medicine and also under Herbal Medicine (to begin with). You then might find titles and authors of articles, along with the name and date of the publication. You may also want to check other headings, such as Health, Herbs, and Healing.

How many volumes do you check? It all depends on the kind of information you are looking for. If you are writing on the history of the medicinal use of herbs in the United States in the past ten years, you obviously will have to scour the *Readers' Guide* for ten years. If all you want is information on the medicinal use of drugs on communes in the 1960s, then probably checking the years 1964 through 1970 would be sufficient. If all you want is information on the herbs used by the president of France on his recent trip to China, all you would need would be the volumes just before, during, and just after his trip.

Since you will encounter many abbreviations in the entries, don't forget to look in front of the *Guide* for any abbreviations you don't understand.

Although the *Readers' Guide* is an indispensable tool, it is doubtful that your school library will subscribe to all the magazines indexed, and even then, it is not going to have every issue of the magazine ever published. You may have to make a trip to a larger library unless your library participates in an interlibrary loan program.

Other Periodical Indexes

The *Readers' Guide* indexes only a percentage of the thousands of periodicals published in the United States. However, for many students like yourself, the *Guide* will be adequate most of the time. In cases where it isn't, you can consult some of the specialized periodical indexes that zero in on a particular field of study.

The information indexed in these guides is much more technical than that found in the *Readers' Guide*.

For instance, publications such as *Time* and *Newsweek* will be indexed in the *Readers' Guide* but not in the *Humanities Index*. On the other hand, articles in the *Bulletin of the Shakespeare Scholars of Tulsa, Oklahoma* (if it existed) might be found in the *Humanities Index* but won't be found in the *Readers' Guide*.

The special indexes will usually be found only in the larger school libraries and in public and college libraries. The actual periodicals will probably be available only in the larger libraries. Even then, you may have to go to microfilm for back issues. Here are some of the more widely used special indexes:

> *Applied Science & Technology Index*
> *Art Index*
> *Biography Index*
> *Biological and Agricultural Index*
> *Book Review Digest*
> *Business Periodical Index*
> *Education Index*
> *General Science Index*
> *Humanities Index*
> *Social Sciences Index*

When you go to the library, you probably will find several or many volumes of a particular index, arranged by date. Assuming you are not doing a historical survey and just want the most recent information on a subject, start with the latest volume and work backward until you find what you are looking for. Just because what you are looking for isn't in one volume doesn't necessarily mean it won't be in another.

On-Line Indexes
You were introduced to on-line indexes in Chapter 3 when you learned how to access data banks to see how many articles were published on your topic. The real

usefulness of these indexes, of course, is not in counting the numbers of articles but in giving you the names and sources of these articles. Data banks such as DIA-LOG and BRS contain information in the sciences, medicine, business, social sciences, and marketing, as well as government reports and much more.

In on-line searching, you can type in key words, and the computer will find all the articles that contain these words. It is necessary, of course, to choose these words carefully, or you would get a large number of irrelevant sources. At the same time, using the wrong words (or not using the right ones) could net you only some of the sources you would use. These data banks are very up-to-date, and a search is done in a fraction of the time it would take manually.

For example, you could specify that you want to find out how vitamin C affects the common cold. You could limit your search to articles published after 1985. You could search a data base that has articles from popular magazines such as *Good Housekeeping* or *Time*, or you could search for the same articles that doctors and scientists might look for. Key words might be *vitamins, vitamin C, colds, viruses,* and *megavitamin therapy.* If you have heard of Linus Pauling, who has done research on this very subject, you could search for articles by or about him as well.

On-line searching should be used only after all the traditional methods of searching out references have been exhausted. If you do conduct an on-line search, here are the steps to follow:

1. Identify the data base or family of data bases to be used—science, humanities, business, etc.
2. List the key words. If a thesaurus of key words is available for your data base, use it. This will be like the list of subject heads in the card catalog and is extremely useful.

3. Decide if you will limit your search by year(s).
4. Decide the type of information you want to receive: bibliography or bibliography and an abstract (a short summary of the article).

The information you get from an on-line search varies with the data base used. For each article, most give the name of the author, the title, the name of the periodical, and an abstract. You still will have to take this information to the periodical section of the library and dig out the actual articles. The abstracts will help you determine whether the articles are worth reading.

You can read the abstracts on the monitor, which is an excellent way of finding out if you are going about your search in the right way. For instance, if all the abstracts you read about vitamin C and colds discuss research on rats only, you obviously need to add a key word or words that indicate you want articles dealing with the effects on human beings (if that indeed is what you want).

The information about the articles can usually be printed out.

On-line searching is a powerful way to access information. Discuss its possibilities with your librarian or media specialist.

INTERVIEWS

Interviews with experts can be valuable. Experts can provide you with the names of the best and most up-to-date books and articles on your topic and can direct you to other sources. You also can do extended interviews to obtain information not otherwise available or available only in technical books and articles.

You could go to the whale expert at the local aquarium and learn things about whales you would have a hard time finding in printed materials. A black artist could probably give you insights on black art that cannot be had elsewhere. Interviews with nurses, doctors, computer programmers, postal clerks, used-car dealers, and architects can provide you with information and points of view unavailable through printed media.

Experts also may be able to help you refine your topic, check your facts, and organize your paper. Naturally you don't want anyone else to write the paper for you, but general recommendations and fact checking won't hurt.

Take careful notes during interviews or ask permission to tape record live interviews. Make sure you cite interviews in your footnotes and list them, along with the time and place they were conducted, in your bibliography.

THE WORKING BIBLIOGRAPHY

6

Now that you know something about different types of reference sources, it is time to put together a working bibliography. The working bibliography consists of all the sources you think you will be using to do your research. It is a working bibliography because as you do your research, you will be adding to this bibliography as you uncover new sources. And when you finish doing your research, you will undoubtedly find that you have not used some or even a lot of the items listed in this bibliography.

By the time you have actually finished writing the paper and are compiling the final bibliography, you probably will find that your initial list has changed considerably.

PRIMARY AND
SECONDARY SOURCES

There are two main kinds of sources: primary and secondary. Primary sources are the original writings of authors, whether novels, nonfiction books, articles, poems, or letters. Government documents such as compilations of unemployment figures or the *Congressional Record* are primary sources, as are transcripts of speeches.

Secondary sources interpret, analyze, paraphrase, and report information contained in primary sources.

For example, in writing on the early development of rock and roll, you will want to go to both primary and secondary sources. You would read the lyrics of Chuck Berry songs, listen to Bo Didley's songs, and read interviews with Elvis Presley (all primary sources); and you would read such critics as Robert Christgau.

Can you be expected to track down, read, and understand a bunch of old speeches, thousand-page volumes of boring statistics, collections of letters written in French, scientific papers obviously written for geniuses, and moldy out-of-print books your library probably won't have? When possible, *try* to look at primary sources. In fact, you may have to.

Let's say one book you are reading mentions another book, by the "leading expert on whale food." You really will have to find this book, if you don't have it on your list anyway. Why read about this expert's work secondhand when you can get it from the horse's mouth!

HOW TO BUILD A BIBLIOGRAPHY

To build a bibliography, you will have to consult the various references discussed in the previous chapter. The only information you should be gathering at this point is the names of books, articles, videotapes, pamphlets, and other documents about your subject.

Start with a visit to your librarian. Mention sources you have already checked or plan to check. Your librarian probably can suggest some other sources.

Check the card catalog for titles of books.

Go to an encyclopedia. If you look at the end of many of the articles, you will find a reading list. Some of these sources may prove useful. Also consult short histories and "concise guides," and books listed on pages 49 to 53 in Chapter 5.

Look in bibliographies on your topic; these may list tens or hundreds of books and articles. Critical bibliographies point out useful points on books on the subject. Books published especially for students may contain useful bibliographies, perhaps of easy-to-understand books and articles.

Check the periodical guides and on-line data bases for titles of relevant articles. Find pamphlets.

Jot down names of people you might want to interview.

LIMIT THE SIZE
OF YOUR BIBLIOGRAPHY

Three factors will automatically limit the number of sources you include in your bibliography: the amount of time you have to complete the assignment, the level of the source or the language it is written in, and the availability of the source.

Because your time is limited, you probably cannot read all the books and articles you find on your topic (unless the amount of available information is extremely limited). Furthermore, at least some of the materials will be too hard or in a language you do not understand. Some of the materials will be unavailable even in the larger libraries near your home.

Two principles will help you make the most of your time and find the most valuable sources.

First, find the best authors in your field. Each subject has recognized authorities, from astrology to punk rock to capital punishment. Take note of names of authors or titles of books that turn up again and again;

read critical bibliographies and bibliographies in textbooks; talk to your teacher or to experts in the field. There is no need, for example, to read all the biographies of John Lennon—only the best ones.

Second, try to use the most recent books and articles. In a field such as astronomy, where there are hundreds of general books, and where theories seem to change monthly, you will want to choose only the most recent books for your paper on quasars. The recent books will incorporate all the earlier material anyway. However, you still may want to read the first accounts of quasars written by their discoverers.

Should you be counting the number of sources used? Do you have to include some of each type of source? The answer is no in both cases, but it is important to include the best sources, from scholarly books to popular articles. Books are comprehensive but less up-to-date than articles. Articles are often more important than books, especially in science.

Choose secondary sources carefully. If you are writing on the life and works of Kate Chopin, the American fiction writer, you will want to include biographies and works of criticism (secondary sources) as well as the most authoritative editions of her own writings. In the case of an author such as Shakespeare, about whom thousands of books have been written, you will have to be selective or you will be reading for the rest of your life.

COMPILING
THE BIBLIOGRAPHY

A good way to compile your list of references is on 3-by-5 index cards.

Each card should contain the name of the author or authors, title of the article or book, date of publication, place of publication (for a book), and name of publisher

Reference number

Author's name

Title of book

7

Jacobs, Francine
Breakthrough : The True Story of Penicillin.
New York : Dodd, Mead, 1985.

City of publication   **Publisher**   **Date of publication**

8

Pringle, Lawrence P.
Ecology.

Number of pages   **Call number**

Date of publication

© 1971 (152 pp)

591.5-P
Brooklyn Pub. Lib.

Library location

Information collected about your sources on index cards is invaluable in doing research and preparing footnotes and the bibliography.

Jacobs, Francine
Breakthrough: The True Story of Penicillin
New York: Dodd, Mead, 1985
7

Pringle, Lawrence P.
Ecology
1971, 152 pp
8
591.5-P
Brooklyn

Author: Jacobs, Francine
Title: Breakthrough: The True Story of Penicillin
Publishing info: New York: Dodd, Mead, 1985
Ref #: 7
Call #:
Library:

Author: Pringle, Lawrence P.
Title: Ecology
Publishing info: 1971, 152 pp
Ref #: 8
Call #: 591.5-P
Library: Brooklyn

These sources were compiled on an Apple IIe computer using AppleWorks. This software combines a data base program with a word processing program and a spreadsheet program (good for preparing charts).

(for a book). The information should be complete and in the same form you will be using when you compile your final bibliography. Chapter 11 instructs you in this.

Also include the catalog number for a book, or a note on the location of the reference in the library. This will enable you to go straight to the reference when you are ready to start your reading.

Arrange the cards alphabetically, by the author's last name. Number each card in one corner—1, 2, 3, and so forth. This will enable you to refer to the source by number on your note cards, saving you a great deal of time and possible writer's cramp.

You also could use a computer to build your list of sources. A data base program would enable you to set up a format for computer "cards."

THE OUTLINE

7

Once you have assembled a working bibliography, you will need to do some more reading so that you can write a more complete outline. Reading in some of the better books on your subject will help you in this endeavor.

Most authors, whether of novels, magazine articles, biographies, scholarly papers, or books, make an outline of what they plan to include in their writing. Many teachers require students to construct outlines before writing term papers. Often the outline must be turned in along with note cards, the working bibliography, rough drafts, and the final paper.

Some people believe that an outline should be very detailed, moving along paragraph by paragraph, with topics, subtopics, and sub-subtopics. Other believe outlines ought just to be as detailed as one needs so that key ideas are not forgotten.

There is no guarantee that doing an outline will automatically lead to a great paper. However, if you haven't written many research papers, feel a little nervous about the process, or have a hard time organizing your material, then consider a fairly detailed outline a requirement—whether or not your teacher makes it one. In case your teacher does not give you an outline format, here's one you might try.

Break up your topic into large pieces. Pretend, for instance, that you are writing a book on the topic and are thinking up chapter divisions. Make a list of these. A computer will come in handy, since you can easily modify the list by changing the entries, inserting new ones, and rearranging them. You may have something like this:

History of black art in America
Names of five main black artists
One section describing the work of each artist
Comparisons of these artists
Is there such a thing as black art?

There are always many ways to organize ideas; it is up to you to decide on the best one. For instance, maybe you would rather begin the outline with the question:

Is there such a thing as black art?

Now you will need to flesh out each heading. For each artist you may want to discuss:

Brief biography
Training
Early influences
Contact with other black artists
First successes
What the critics say
Views on black art

You can insert this list under the appropriate general "chapter" in your outline. You may number the chapters or simply use line breaks, indents, underlining, or boldface type to mark the distinctions. The outline in the box below may be what you're used to doing.

I. History of black art in America
II. Artist number 1
   A. Training
   B. Early influences
   C. Contact with other black artists
   D. First successes
      1. Show at Art Institute of Chicago in 1965
      2. Exhibit at Museum of Modern Art in 1968
      3. Exhibit at Jones Gallery in 1970
   E. What the critics say
   F. Views on black art
III. Artist number 2
   (etc.)

Once you have such an outline, you probably will want to flesh it out even more and perhaps add some little notes:

First successes:

Mention three
Discuss Museum of Modern Art exhibit in 1968
Don't forget to mention joint show with Warhol

You also may want to indicate the amount of space you think you'll want to spend:

First successes (250 words)

or:

First successes:

    Exhibit (two paragraphs)
    Warhol show (short paragraph)

You can, of course, map out your paper paragraph by paragraph, but this may be excessive. It may prevent you from developing a writing style, may make the final paper sound like a succession of disconnected paragraphs, and will definitely inhibit you from thinking as you write. Most writers develop their ideas as they write; they don't just fill in the blanks.

Once again, your instructor may want something different, or you may have done it differently in the past and want to do this outline the way you have done all the others. Just keep in mind that an outline is simply a tool to help you write better.

TAKING NOTES

8

Once you have located the sources you intend to use for your research and have prepared your outline to guide you in your research, it is time to go through the sources and take notes.

HOW TO READ,
WHAT TO NOTE

Take notes while you are reading. Do not read a source and make notes from memory. Approach each source with your topic clearly in mind and know exactly what you want from that source.

If you are writing on Wyatt Earp and have selected two book-length biographies and ten articles on his social contributions, you may be able to derive all the necessary biographical information from the biographies and ignore the biographical information in the articles—unless they are not mentioned in the books.

In reading each source you may notice much of the same material—especially in biographies and in popular articles. Once you take down a piece of information from source A, there is no need to note the same information from source B.

Read slowly and note only information pertinent to your topic. This usually requires a lot of sifting. For example, you may read a long article on whales and find only one sentence of value. Another book may yield fifty pieces of information.

As you read, you may come across conflicting information. One book says your subject was born in France; another says it was in Germany. You also will find points you aren't sure of or can't find answers to, or you may wonder about some aspect of your topic. Jot down these notes and questions on slips of paper or cards, perhaps of a different color from the other slips of paper and cards. Or put a symbol in one corner, like a question mark or the word NOTE or QUESTION. As you read further, the answers may pop up. If they don't, additional research is necessary.

TAKE NOTES ON CARDS
OR ON A COMPUTER

Unless your teacher specifies otherwise, take notes on 3-by-5 or 4-by-6 cards. (Some people prefer slips of paper of this size instead.)

Do not make notes in books or tear out pages of books or magazines. Photocopy materials in the library if you prefer doing some of your note taking at home. You may want copies of key articles, reading lists, or chapters for quick reference.

You also can take notes on a computer, using a data base program and a computer. Data base programs have many names: filing programs, data base managers, indexers, notebook programs. They should be able to handle a large amount of data, break it down

NOTE

read more on 19th century black artists in Boston

NOTE

Check birthdate of FDR (again!)

Jot down notes to yourself
on note cards.

in several categories (called fields), sort it by these fields, then print it out.

Once these fields are set up (and on some programs an actual note card can be placed on the screen), you fill them in, one by one, with your notes, sort it by these fields, then print it out. You can use your data base program to print out your information in different arrangements, too. For example, you can construct and alphabetize your sources by the author's last name, and you could group together information of a similar nature.

You may want to try using special computer software such as *Term Paper Writer* (published by Personal Choice Software in Mountain View, California), which contains a word processing program and can also help you take notes, prepare an outline, and compile your footnotes and bibliography.

TAKE NOTES SYSTEMATICALLY

Write the number of the reference in one corner of the card. If you don't want to use numbers, write down the abbreviated title of the work instead:

> *Gibbon, The Decline and Fall of the Roman Empire, volume 8*
> *Decline & Fall, vol. 8*

or

> *Gibbon, vol. 8*

Put down one fact, group of closely related facts, or main ideas on each card. This way you can easily organize your information when you write the paper. You will be able to organize the cards quickly, weed out duplicate material, and discard and insert material without having to hunt through a lot of scribbling on each.

p 44, 46, 48, 80

Dancers train 16 hr day in USSR,
only 8 in US. They are trained ①
from early age, paid for by state.
One dancer said she hated
training. Famous old dancers
toured a lot.

TRAINING

---

p. 44 ①

Dancers train 16 hr/day
in USSR, only 8 in US

TRAINING

When taking notes from sources, put one fact
on each card, as shown on the bottom card.
The top card contains too much information.
On each card write the topic (TRAINING), the
source number (1), and the page in the
source from which the fact is taken (p. 44).

LEARN NOTE CARD MAKER

NOTE CARD MAKER organizes information
from research.

It STORES your information, and then
allows you to...

    SELECT pieces of information
    you want, or

    SORT your information the way
    you choose.

Press SPACE BAR to go on.

NOTE CARDS

Which would you like to do?
1 Create a NOTE CARD FILE
2 Edit NOTE CARDS
3 Search NOTE CARDS
4 Go to BIBLIOGRAPHY
5 Delete a FILE

6 Return to DISK MENU

Press 1, 2, 3, 4, 5, or 6.

Note Card Maker *is a program that enables you
to include a computer (in this case an Apple
IIe) in the note-taking process. The program*

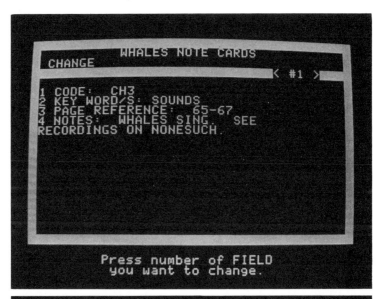

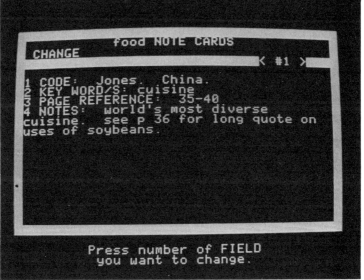

has a teaching section and numerous menus. With this software you can sort your "cards" by reference (CODE) or key words (KEYWORD/S).

You might put down the definition of oceanography on one card, the names of its six pioneers on another card, one main achievement of each pioneer on each of six cards, and so forth. When writing the paper, you may want to use only three achievements, so it will be easy to ignore three of the cards. Had you put all this information on one card, you would have had a lot more work to do separating the useful from the useless information. It also is easier to neatly jot down a few words at a time on one card than many sentences.

Add to each card the page number or numbers of each source you draw material from, even if you are neither paraphrasing nor quoting. This makes it easy to go back and check your facts, add material, and document borrowed ideas.

Give each card a topic code as you go along. For instance, in your research on whales, you decide on five sections: whaling, whaling operations, economics of whaling today, the morality of whaling, and Greenpeace. As you go through a reference and find information on one of these topics, you would code the information: HISTORY, OPERATIONS, ECONOMICS, MORALITY, GP. This would go in one of the blank corners of your note card, perhaps circled.

Write legibly. If you don't, you will get the facts wrong and may have to re-research some of the information. Using abbreviations is okay so long as you can decipher them later. Note them on a card or piece of paper.

Why code your cards? Because when you finish going through your references, you can easily sort the cards for each source by subject instead, then organize each subject by arranging the cards until the order you want is achieved.

When you finish taking notes from one source, whether it is one note or one hundred, put a rubber band around the card or cards and put a card on top with the reference information abbreviated. That way you know which pile is which.

ACKNOWLEDGE OTHER PEOPLE'S IDEAS

There is a right way to extract information from a source—and a wrong way.

The right way is to either take notes in your own words or put quotes around the words of the author you are taking down. If your wording is *close* to that of the author, use quotes but make a note on the card saying "paraphrase." To paraphrase is to put someone else's ideas into your own words. Put quotations or paraphrases on note cards in the same way that you were shown above. Indicating the page number(s) is mandatory.

When the time comes to turn your notes into paragraphs, you will cite, in footnotes or notes at the back of your paper, the sources of other people's ideas, even if you express these ideas in your own words.

Not giving credit where credit is due is *plagiarism.*

Plagiarism is against the law, it is cheating, and it is unethical—that is, it goes against the whole idea that students should be doing their own work. In college, plagiarism may lead to expulsion from school. Even if you do not deliberately steal from another author, you will be accused of plagiarism if you use someone else's wording or ideas without having given that person due credit.

When and How to Paraphrase or Use Quotations

Use quotations sparingly. They are especially useful (1) when the other author says something so effectively or beautifully that you want to capture the language of the original, (2) to lend authority on the subject quoted, and

(3) in a critical paper, where you discuss someone else's writing.

Paraphrasing is handy when you want to condense someone else's important ideas or add a touch of authority to your paper. Here is a passage from an imaginary book by the famous imaginary social critic I. M. Short:

> Society as a whole should take responsbility for the derelicts, junkies, and other outcasts rather than blame them and then incarcerate them. Is it their fault that they were born into poverty, or were victims of discrimination, or were simply unable to cope with unemployment and too large families? No, of course not. Society must assume much of the blame for their lot and correct their lot rather than punish the victims.

Here is your paraphrase on the note card:

> Short would put much of the blame for addiction and dereliction on society rather than on the individuals themselves, whom he sees as victims.

The paraphrase is brief. It summarizes Short's views. It is in the paraphraser's own words. It is not just the original quotation with a few words changed, or the sentence order changed. The paraphraser has understood Short's meaning, then restated it.

TAKE NOTES ON POSSIBLE ILLUSTRATIONS

If you see charts, tables, photographs, diagrams, cartoons, or drawings you may want to include redrawn or photocopied in your paper, note their sources the way you have been noting other information. You will need to credit the sources when the time comes.

A LITTLE LECTURE
ON WRITING

9

Before you begin the actual writing of your paper, you might benefit from a little lecture on writing. It is a "little lecture" because everyone hates lectures, especially long ones.

After speaking, writing is the most important form of communication in our society. Everywhere we turn, we see words in print, from gum wrappers to newspapers and books, from cereal boxes to television commercials. In doing your term paper, you are joining the ranks of all those writers contributing to the enormous flood of written and printed words that continually drowns our daily lives.

Even though your paper is only a requirement and your topic probably of little interest to anyone but yourself and your teacher, why not pretend you are writing for a wider audience? Why not imagine you are going to send your paper to a popular magazine or to a scholarly journal, or that you are going to read it in front of an audience composed of your fellow students, or perhaps composed of the people from college admissions offices?

In other words, since you are going to all this work to dig up facts and organize them into something meaningful, why not put some energy also into the way you express yourself? While it is true that except for an English class, a decently written, well-organized, and well-thought-out term paper will get you a good grade, a paper that also is well written will snare you that A or A+ in a flash. That is because teachers appreciate good writing, and because so often good writing is associated with good everything else, for example good organization.

Writing well requires effort and practice, of course, so let's spend just a little time looking at some of the characteristics of good writing and some of the things to consider while you write.

AUDIENCE

Each audience is different: soap opera lovers watching commercials, match cover readers, readers of *Time* magazine and of the *National Enquirer*, of Shakespeare and of Judy Blume, of shampoo labels and instructions for using computer software. As a writer, you have to consider your audience and write for it.

In your case, the main audience is your teacher, but if you think only of your teacher, the result will be very narrow, too private. Think of your teacher as being part of a larger audience composed of intelligent readers. Their degree of sophistication depends in part on the subject. While your teacher may know something about your subject, it is better to pretend that he or she doesn't. This will prevent you from becoming too specialized. By assuming intelligence, you will avoid being too simplistic.

For example, in writing a paper on whales for a biology class, you can assume that your teacher understands the general principles of biology and knows a little about a lot of animals. You can also assume that your teacher probably knows little about whales. You needn't define migration, but you will need to discuss the specifics of whale migration.

STYLE AND TONE

Such considerations will affect your style and tone.

Since you are not writing for whale experts, you shouldn't adopt the remote, formal, stilted, dry tone of the specialist writing for other specialists. You can see this kind of writing in professional journals. Although precise language is always welcomed, these specialists are going to be as bored by the writing of these articles as you or your teacher would be reading them. The difference is that the specialist *has* to read the articles to keep up with developments in the field; if the article is well written, perhaps even a little entertaining, fine; if it's not, well, it's to be expected.

Conversely, too informal a style and too friendly a tone are inappropriate for the conveyance of hard scientific facts. Since your teacher is more like a reader of a magazine like *Time* or *Science News*, or of a general-interest history publication, it is appropriate to be somewhat relaxed and even to allow yourself some humor or other flights of the imagination.

This is especially appropriate with a paper on a literary figure or work, where good writing is valued more than in the sciences. Injecting a joke into a report of your scientific experimentation is probably unacceptable, unless the joke fits in with the purpose of the experiment.

Avoid jargon, even in technical writing. Jargon is a collection of specialized terms used by practitioners of certain disciplines. While jargon is a useful shorthand, its use has led to the enormous gap that now exists between the general public and the specialists in various fields, and more recently between specialists in different branches of the same field! The neuropsychologists can no longer be understood by the neurosurgeons or by the behavioral psychologists!

LANGUAGE

Words are the building blocks of writing. How they are used is obviously what determines the way your ideas will be received.

While dry writing is boring, flowery language—using a lot of modifiers—is equally offensive. As usual, the middle ground often is the most successful.

Plants inhabiting the littoral zone often extrude themselves onto composites ten to twenty meters from the next zone.

A myriad of extraordinarily lovely and breathtakingly colorful plants that have spent years establishing their homeland in the magical zone between high and low tides remarkably often creep longingly onto the bric-a-brac but massive boulders a mere ten to twenty meters from the zone of conifers and other symmetrical organisms.

Plants such as seaweeds that normally live between high and low tides often grow higher up on the shore, sometimes as far as the trees in places like Big Sur.

The first example is dry, the second flowery, and the third simple and accessible. Use technical terms only when their meaning cannot easily be "translated."

SENTENCE STRUCTURE

Most writing is composed of sentences. They are important building blocks of writing.

Most good expository writing—writing that explains—uses a combination of sentences of different lengths. Variety is the spice of both life and good writing. Try mixing up short, long, medium, very long, and extremely short sentences. Sentences that are all very short will make your writing sound like *Dick and Jane* readers. A sequence of extraordinarily long sentences will confuse your reader. And a conglomeration of medium-length sentences will bore your reader.

Use the active voice primarily. The passive voice is weak. In the active voice, the subject is acting. In the passive voice, something is being acted upon by the subject.

Passive: Migration is done by whales.

Active: Whales migrate.

Passive: The fast-draw was used by Wyatt Earp at the OK Corral to kill the Daltons.

Active: Wyatt Earp used the fast-draw at the OK Corral to kill the Daltons.

Notice that fewer words are used in the examples using the active voice.

Sentence openings are strong and weak, too, depending on whether the subject leads off a sentence or is buried within:

Weak: In whale migration, the whales move south in the winter.

Strong: Migrating whales move south in winter.

Although writing that always begins with the subject can be effective in fiction (for example, in the writing of Ernest Hemingway and Richard Wright), it would be monotonous in the kind of writing you are doing. So begin some sentences with prepositional phrases and subordinate clauses:

In order to better understand the plight of the black artist, we . . .

Although Soviet cars are poorly made, they . . .

In Hamlet, *Shakespeare . . .*

A certain number of sentences using the passive voice is also not a bad thing and in fact will be inevitable: some ideas need to be expressed in this way.

PARAGRAPH STRUCTURE

Paragraphs are the major building blocks of types of writing like term papers. They express a group of related ideas, or flesh out one small idea. Vary the length of your paragraphs in the same way that you vary the length of your sentences. One-sentence paragraphs are effective—when not overused.

Use them to emphasize certain points.

There are strong paragraphs, and weak ones, as with sentences. "Strong" paragraphs state the main idea of the paragraph at the beginning or at the end. "Weak" ones bury the main idea in the middle.

Although you probably have learned all about topic sentences, a great deal of writers do not use topic sentences in their paragraphs. In fact, many paragraphs in magazine articles are loosely constructed. Paragraphs often have one main idea, but in magazines such as

The New Yorker, some paragraphs might contain enough ideas to make your English teacher scream.

Unless you feel very confident in your writing, avoid huge paragraphs, and make your paragraph's main idea very apparent—which usually means putting it at or near the beginning of a paragraph.

THE FIRST PERSON

Is it okay to write in the first person? There are times in this book where I have wanted to use the first person, but I have avoided doing so because it has seemed inappropriate.

The preceding paragraph could have been re-phrased to avoid the first person: "There are times in this book when use of the first person seemed called for, but its use always seemed inappropriate as well."

There may be times when *I* is indeed called for, but think long and hard before actually going ahead and using it.

Now that you know a little more about some of the qualities of good writing, it is finally time to write!

ORGANIZING YOUR INFORMATION AND WRITING THE ROUGH DRAFT

10

At this stage, writing means writing a first—or rough — draft of your paper. You will be combining ideas and facts from your different sources and getting these ideas to flow in a smooth, organized fashion.

Keep in mind the points made in the little lecture on writing, but be more concerned with content and organization than with style. That is why this first version of your paper is called a rough draft. Don't worry too much now about breaking up your paper into formal sections. You will polish your writing and attend to organizational details later.

If you have followed the steps outlined in the previous chapters, you should be in pretty good shape at this point. You will have the bulk of your cards in little (or big) piles organized by reference. You also may have a small pile of notes to yourself: "Don't forget to highlight the fact that Greenpeace does such and such," or "Not sure about Wyatt Earp's birthplace."

SORT AND ORGANIZE
YOUR NOTE CARDS

The first thing to do with your note cards—or data base fields—is to sort them by subject. If you have coded the cards by subject already, your task will be relatively easy.

Now organize the cards in each subject pile according to the order of subtopics in your outline. For instance, if you are writing on black American artists, now is the time to pull all the cards on the five artists and to arrange them by show, views, childhood, training, and so forth.

In sorting your cards, you may decide you want to rearrange the order. Don't do this yet. Just make a note on a card and put the card in front of the card or group of cards you may want to rearrange: "Move before last section?" When you have sorted all the cards according to your original order, *then* change the order. But first rearrange the outline, which is your master plan. Your task will be a breeze if you wrote the outline using your word processor.

While sorting the cards the first time, you will undoubtedly see gaps in your information. You might write on a card, slipped in with the others, "Add date of sister's birth here," or "Tell why blue whales need more food per ton of body weight than other animals."

If you answered questions jotted down earlier and have a pile of miscellaneous cards, now is the time to insert these cards into their proper places in the stacks of cards arranged according to the outline. Toss out the notes to yourself once you have handled the matter, set aside oddball cards, discard duplicates, tag cards still containing contradictory information, and do anything else necessary to streamline and solidify your notes. Try to clear up problems, at this point, but don't stall because of one or two dates—provided, of course, they are not essential parts of your argument.

WRITE THE PAPER

You are now ready to write the paper, following the order of your note cards (which is the same as that of your outline).

Begin a new paragraph each time you present a new main idea. Use section headings to separate large blocks of related material (although you may not wish to keep these headings in the final draft). Feel free to squeeze in as many facts and ideas as you can, even if you decide later to eliminate some of them. Although it is not that hard to add material later, it is probably easier to cut material.

If you have taken notes using a data base program, use the computer to group your electronic note cards by topic. Arrange the topics in the order in which you plan to write about them. With a printout of your ordered "cards," you essentially have the skeleton of your term paper. You then need to expand and connect the paragraphs.

If your data base program and word processing program are compatible, you can transfer the information in the data base to the word processing program. This will save you a step, and your "skeleton" will be ready to work on, without your having to retype or re-word-process it. An integrated-software package—one that combines a word processing program with a data base program—can be used instead of separate programs.

Some word processors are easier to use than others. The more efficient ones allow you to work with two or more files at once. You could display your outline at the bottom of the screen while composing the paper at the top. You could also use the file at the bottom as an electronic notepad while you are working at the top. You also might be able to display your notes and writing in progress at the same time, facilitating the insertion of quotations.

You may feel better about working on hard copy (printout). Print everything out, including what might be a very rough copy, with extrawide margins and double or triple spacing, and make your notes and changes just as you would if you were writing longhand or typing.

INTEGRATE AND ACKNOWLEDGE OTHER PEOPLE'S MATERIAL

You have included quotations and paraphrases of authors on your note cards. When writing the first draft, you must be absolutely clear in your use of this material. Keep only those quotes that really add to your paper. Beware of using too many quotations: you will not get a medal for your efforts.

Incorporate short quotations into the sentence or paragraph, with the number at the end:

Dodge City, for example, was first a military post. Later, it became a post for buffalo hunters, but before the Chisolm Trail was established, it became almost deserted. "Then, when the longhorns from Texas were driven north to the railroad at Dodge, the town became an A number one cow town."[1] Dodge had been a city of lawless and violent men. . . .

Indent longer quotations and type or word-process them in a block style; introduce them by citing part of the reference:

Animosities remaining from the Civil War apparently contributed to the violence of the cow towns. According to Dane Coolidge in Fighting Men of the West:

*The bloody feud between the peace offi-
cers who ruled Dodge City, and the cow-
boys who came up the trail, was a result
in large measure of a post-war bitter-
ness, stirred up by rattlesnakes and
whiskey. The South had lost, and the
impoverished Texans began driving their
cattle north. But at the Kansas line they
encountered their old enemies wearing
badges on their vests.[2]*

Handle paraphrased material, and quotations that are
incomplete sentences, as follows:

*According to Jones,[3] Wyatt Earp didn't like guns
even though he was a famous gunfighter. This
goes against the standard image of Earp, which,
according to another authority, "is undoubtedly
correct, small doubts notwithstanding."[4]*

Number footnotes and put them at the bottom of the
page on which the quote or paraphrase occurs, or else
create "endnotes"—a section that eventually will go at
the end of the paper. Follow your teacher's instructions.

If you put the footnote on the same page as the
quotation or paraphrase, single-space it (at least in the
final draft), and insert a blank line between it and the
text. Skip lines between notes if you have more than
one. Endnotes can be single- or double-spaced; follow
your teacher's instructions.

Figuring out how much room to leave at the bottom
of the page for footnotes is tricky. Using a word processor can simplify this task. Either way, you will have to
count lines of text and footnotes and do some estimat-
ing. Chapter 11 shows you the correct form for a footnote.

2

towns was directly related to the periodic arrival of Texas
cowhands bringing their herds to the Kansas rail stations for
shipment to eastern markets. After spending long, lonely weeks
sweating and eating dust in the Great Plains sun, the cowboy
arrived in the cowtown: "He was free now - unemployed,
uninhibited, and rich - until tomorrow or next week. They were
ready to raise hell."[1] Of course, all kinds of human vultures,
gamblers, cowmen, prostitutes, and other sharp operators were
waiting for them.

Animosities remaining from the Civil War apparently
contributed to the violence in the cowtowns. According to
Dane Coolidge in Fighting Men of the West:

> The bloody feud between the peace officers who
> ruled Dodge City, and the cowboys who came up the
> trail, was a result in large measure of a post-war
> bitterness, stirred up by rattlesnake whiskey. The
> South had lost, and the impoverished Texans began
> driving their cattle north. But at the Kansas line
> they encountered their old enemies wearing badges
> on their vests.[2]

The purpose of this paper is to discuss frontier justice,
focusing on the cowtowns of Kansas City and two of the most
renowned peace officers, Bat Masterson and Wyatt Earp.

---

[1] Nyle H. Miller and Joseph W. Snell, Great Gunfighters of
the Kansas Cowtowns (Kansas: University of Nebraska Press, 1963),
p. 3.

[2] Dane Coolidge, Fighting Men of the West (New York: Books
for Libraries Press, 1932), p. 72.

Paraphrase Correctly

You already know a little about paraphrasing, but this technique confuses even the best of writers.

You can paraphrase an author's general views on a subject. You might say:

Jones seems to argue that Wyatt Earp didn't like guns.[5]

Or you can paraphrase a specific passage. Here is such a passage, followed by two paraphrases:

Then, when the longhorns from Texas were driven north to the railroad terminal at Dodge, the town became an A number one cow town.

Paraphrase 1:

When the cattle from Texas were driven to the terminal at Dodge, the town became a number one cow town.

This is a paraphrase, yes, but a bad one because it is too close to the original. You may as well quote the original.

Paraphrase 2:

According to Johnson, Dodge became a first-class cow town after the cattle were driven there from Texas.

Sample page from a term paper on Wyatt Earp written by a student at the author's school

Watch out that your paper doesn't turn into a mass of footnoted paraphrases; this is as bad as a paper over-burdened with quotations.

Perhaps the only exception is when you are analyzing the work of another author. In discussing Richard Wright's *Native Son,* you might want to use quite a few quotes from the book.

WRITE CREATIVE
BEGINNINGS AND ENDINGS

One of the hardest parts of writing any paper is writing the beginning. Many authors may write the opening last, and may rewrite it more times than they rewrite the rest of their article, paper, or book.

Your opening can be something standard, like, "In this paper . . ." or something a little snappier: "Wyatt Earp is not the man you thought he was. He was not a ruthless killer, a fearless fighter, a lover of violence. He actually hated violence."

The latter opening, followed by a presentation of your ideas, more closely resembles openings for articles in magazines, called *leads.* The lead is meant to grab the reader's attention and at the same time set forth the main idea of the article.

While your teacher may disapprove of something too catchy for an opening, he or she will probably appreciate an opening that is more original than "This paper will examine the relationship between Wyatt Earp and his mother and investigate how it contributed to his hatred of violence." In writing such an opening, you will at best be guaranteed a sigh or groan from your teacher. Why not surprise your teacher, then, with something a little different!

Read some different types of openings in books, magazine articles, newspaper stories, journal articles, and so on, to see what you like and don't like.

Here are a few more sample openings of both kinds:

Soccer is played and watched by more people in the world than any other sport. It is also the fastest-growing participation sport in the United States. Let's take a closer look at why so many people like this game.

The popularity of soap operas has risen tremendously over the past few years. At present, in fact, nine of the ten programs most often recorded on home VCRs are soap operas. Why are soap operas so popular?

In Europe it has been said that architecture is the one art to which Americans have made original contributions of the first rank. In the past seventy years American architecture has greatly influenced the design of European buildings. Yet the architect who most influenced American architecture has never received full credit for his contribution. This architect, of course, is Louis Sullivan.

The same approach applies to conclusions.

Traditionally, the ending of a term paper provides you a chance to tie things up neatly and perhaps draw conclusions from your research. You also could express what you learned that you didn't know before. A conclusion can be one paragraph or several.

If you do it this way, go right ahead—you won't be faulted by your teacher. You should know, however, that all an ending really has to do is . . . end. If you can think of a better way to conclude than to summarize, why not try to!

Your teacher will be falling asleep over the fifteenth paper that ends, ''In this paper, we saw that Wyatt Earp hated violence because he loved his mother. In conclusion, it is only fair to state that . . . " when along comes your snappy ending to jolt her out of her chair with a smile of relief: "The question of whether Earp loved his mother so much that he gave up gunfighting is bound to be one that infuriates the non-Freudian historians of the Old West for years to come." This certainly sounds like a conclusion, but it adds something extra—a challenge.

Other examples of conclusions:

The overwhelming evidence shows that drinking and driving don't mix. This paper will have heightened the reader's awareness of what can happen when they do.

There is little we can do once a nuclear attack occurs. The strategy the world must take is to avoid one at all costs.

In the last example, the first sentence summarizes the contents of the paper (evidence that little can be done once a nuclear attack occurs), while the second sentence offers the author's considered opinion. It is a strongly stated opinion, too, as evidenced by the word *must.*

Look in magazines and newspapers for some ideas on ending your paper, but don't be surprised if you find that half the articles and stories have a cute ending, a twist, or no ending whatsoever!

You may have to revise your opening and conclusion several times to get them just right.

PREPARE THE BIBLIOGRAPHY

Prepare a rough draft of your bibliography at this stage, even though you later may add or delete some of the entries.

There are different types of bibliographies, and your teacher may specify the kind he or she wants:

1. All sources consulted are included, whether or not you actually used anything from them in the paper—for example, a quotation.
2. Only sources also cited in footnotes are included.
3. All sources cited in footnotes are included, along with other, selected sources.
4. None of the above.

If your teacher doesn't tell you the kind to do, try (1), which covers all the basics.

In the next chapter you will find the correct forms to use for the entries in your bibliography.

HOW TO CITE
REFERENCE SOURCES

11

Footnotes must be constructed in a certain way. So must the bibliography. The reason is so that people reading your paper will know the source of your ideas and facts—when that source is other than you.

FOOTNOTE FORMAT

Each type of reference is listed in a slightly different way. The following formats are acceptable to many people. Your teacher may suggest another way to do this, however. Be sure to follow exactly the spacing, punctuation, and order of each of the parts of the citation.

BOOKS WITH
ONE AUTHOR

[1]Author's first name Author's last name, Title (place of publication: publisher, copyright date), pages used.

Example:

[1]Carl W. Breihan, Great Gunfighters of the West (New York: New American Library, 1981), pp. 45-46.

BOOKS WITH TWO AUTHORS

[2]First Author's first name First Author's last name and Second Author's first name Second Author's last name, Title (place of publication: publisher, copyright date), pages used.

Example:

[2]John H. Brown and William S. Speer, Encyclopedia of the New West (Easley, S.C.: Southern Historical Press, 1978), p. 187.

NO AUTHOR GIVEN

[3]Title (place of publication: publisher, copyright date), pages used.

Example:

[3]Personalities of the West and Midwest (New York: American Biographical Institute, 1985), p. 462.

INSTITUTION, ASSOCIATION, ETC., AS AUTHOR

[4]Institution, Title (place of publication: publisher, copyright date), pages used.

Example:

[4]Western Writers of America. Water Trails West (New York: Avon, 1979), pp. 101-102.

EDITOR AS AUTHOR

[5]Editor's first name Editor's last name, ed., Title (place of publication, copyright date), pages used.

Example:

[5]Jerome O. Steffan, ed., The American West: New Perspectives. New Dimensions (Norman: University of Oklahoma Press, 1979), p. 15.

ENCYCLOPEDIA ARTICLE— SIGNED

[6]Name of encyclopedia, year of edition, s.v. "Title of article," by Author's first name Author's last name.

Example:

[6]Encyclopedia Britannica, 1978 ed., s.v. "History of the United States," by Forrest McDonald.

ENCYCLOPEDIA ARTICLE— UNSIGNED

[7]Name of encyclopedia, year of edition, s.v. "Title of article."

Example:

[7]Collier's Encyclopedia, 1981 ed., s.v. "Earp, Wyatt."

ARTICLE
IN MAGAZINE

[8]Author's first name Author's last name, "Title of article," Name of magazine volume number of magazine (date of magazine): page number.

Example:

[8]Peter Lyon, "The Wild, Wild West," American Heritage 11 (August 1960): p. 42

PAMPHLETS,
GOVERNMENT
DOCUMENTS

[9]Name of agency, Title of pamphlet, date of publication, pages.

Example:

[9]U.S. Department of Justice, The United State Marshals' Service, Then...and Now, October 1978, p. 3.

INTERVIEWS

[10]Interview with First name of person interviewed Last name of person interviewed, organization, place of interview, date of interview.

Example:

[10]Interview with Claire Hertz, Wyoming Historical Society, Cheyenne, 21 August, 1986.

More information on format can be found in the following books:

Chicago Manual of Style, 13th ed. Chicago: University of Chicago Press, 1984.

Turabian, Kate L. *A Manual for Writers of Term Papers, Theses, and Dissertations*, 5th ed. Chicago: University of Chicago Press, 1987.

BIBLIOGRAPHY FORMAT

Bibliographies are styled slightly differently. The main difference is that authors' names are always listed last name, first; periods are used instead of commas between units of the listing; parentheses are not used for the publication data for books; and page numbers are not used.,

Here is a preliminary example, first for a footnote, then for a bibliographic entry:

[7]Carl Sagan, Cosmos (New York: Random House, 1980), pp. 56-57.

Sagan, Carl. Cosmos. New York: Random House, 1980.

The information provided in a bibliographic entry enables the reader to easily find and evaluate the source.

Here is a list of formats. More can be found in the two books listed at the end of the previous section.

BOOKS WITH
ONE AUTHOR

Author's last name, Author's first name. Title. Place of publication: publisher, copyright date.

Example:

Breihan, Carl W. Great Gunfighters of the
West. New York: New American Library,
1981.

BOOKS WITH
TWO AUTHORS

First Author's last name, First Author's
first name, and Second Author's last
name, Second Author's first name.
Title. Place of publication: publisher,
copyright date.

Example:

Brown, John H., and Speer, William S.
Encyclopedia of the New West. Easley,
S.C.: Southern Historical Press, 1978.

NO AUTHOR
GIVEN

Title. Place of publication: publisher,
copyright date.

Example:

Personalities of the West and Midwest. New
York: American Biographical Institute,
1985.

INSTITUTION,
ASSOCIATION, ETC.,
AS AUTHOR

Institution. Title. Place of publication:
publisher, copyright date.

Example:

Western Writers of America. Water Trails
West. New York: Avon, 1979.

EDITOR AS AUTHOR

Editor's last name, Editor's first name,
ed. Title. Place of publication:
publisher, copyright date.

Example:

Steffan, Jerome O., ed. The American West.
Norman: University of Oklahoma Press,
1979.

ENCYCLOPEDIA ARTICLE—
SIGNED

Name of encyclopedia, year ed. s.v. "Title
of article," by Author's first
name Author's last name.

Example:

Encyclopedia Britannica, 1978 ed. s.v.
"History of the United States," by
Forrest McDonald.

ENCYCLOPEDIA ARTICLE—
UNSIGNED

Name of Encyclopedia, year ed. s.v. "Title
of article."

Example:

Collier's Encyclopedia, 1981 ed. s.v.
"Earp, Wyatt."

ARTICLE
IN MAGAZINE

Author's last name, Author's first name.
"Title of article." Name of magazine,
date of magazine, pages used.

Example:

Lyon, Peter. "The Wild, Wild West."
American Heritage, August 1960,
pp. 45-46.

PAMPHLETS,
GOVERNMENT
DOCUMENTS

Name of agency. Title of pamphlet, date.

Example:

U.S. Department of Justice. The United
States Marshals' Service, Then...and
Now, October 1978.

INTERVIEW

Last name of person interviewed, First
    name of person interviewed.
    Organization, place of interview, date
    of interview.

Example:

Hartz, Claire. Wyoming Historical
    Society, Cheyenne, 21 August 1986.

REVISING THE ROUGH DRAFT; WRITING THE FINAL DRAFT

12

A rough draft is just that: a rough draft. The idea was to get your ideas down on paper in approximately the form you wanted them to take.

Writing from your note cards or computer "cards" sounded easy: Just construct a string of paragraphs, follow a few of the suggestions on writing, add a beginning and an ending, and bingo, a brilliant term paper. As you may have found out, writing a good rough draft involved a bit more effort.

MAKING REVISIONS

After writing the rough draft, read it. Read it critically, but also try to be nice to yourself. If you are too critical, you will feel discouraged. If you think the first draft is just wonderful and needs no additional work, you probably are deluding yourself. Almost all writers revise.

Some writers revise very little. They feel good about the first draft, may make a few changes, and will indeed wind up with a good piece of writing. This goes for both students and professional writers. Other writers revise the first draft quite a lot, retype (or re-word-process), and are happy with the second draft. But a lot of writers, both students and professionals, revise more. They may do two or three or four or even more drafts.

It is not the number of drafts that matters but the quality of the writing and the quality of the revisions. If you know how to revise and know good writing, you will be on the road to writing a good term paper.

The best way to be able to recognize the qualities of good writing is to read a lot, and to read both good and bad writing. Your English teacher should be able to give you suggestions. By studying both good and bad writing and comparing it with your own writing, you will be able to determine how good your first draft is and how much revising is necessary to turn it into a piece of good writing.

Most students don't revise enough. With this in mind, you will be able to streak ahead of your fellow students by revising a little more than you normally might be inclined to.

READ FOR CONTENT

Read your paper once again, this time more carefully.

Do you have enough information in it so that your presentation is clear and complete? Have you written enough or too much? Are your ideas and facts all there? Are they well organized? Are there gaps or unanswered questions? Make notes in the margin: "Why did he shoot his friend?" "Add details of his trip to Paris." "Explain quarks more clearly." You may have to search your notes for the necessary information or even return to the library to do additional research.

Go back now and make the required changes. Using a word processor will make your task easier than

Although most research ~~for term papers~~
is done in libraries, research also
can be done through interviews,
experimentation, and surveys.
Sometimes, ~~in fact,~~ the best way to
learn about a new field ~~(like~~
~~cryptozoology)~~ is to talk to an
expert. Still, most of your research
will ~~involve information gathered from~~ be with
printed matter. ~~and, in some cases,~~
~~from computers, video disks,~~
~~filmstrips, videotapes, and other~~
~~media.~~

Your term paper is probably not
going to win you a Pulitzer Prize, ~~or a~~
~~Nobel Prize,~~ although it might be the
first step in a career leading to one.
But you <u>will</u> learn how to think and
how to work with information. These
~~extremely~~ are important ~~talents~~ abilities in ~~an age~~ our

Even final drafts can be revised further.
This material, without the revisions done here,
will probably sound familiar to you.

if you typed or used pen and pencil for the first draft. Either way, you will need to add, delete, and shift the order of material. If you don't have a computer, you will have made your job easier by leaving lots of space between lines in the rough draft; for typists this means triple-spacing and leaving large margins. You may have to cut and paste to insert and rearrange whole paragraphs.

Now read the paper with an eye toward continuity, paying special attention to transitions.

STRENGTHEN TRANSITIONS

A collection of paragraphs containing one idea per paragraph and linked in accordance with your outline will probably wind up sounding like a series of disconnected ideas. What's missing? Why, of course: transitions.

You need to connect your paragraphs so that ideas flow smoothly. To do this you may have to add or subtract paragraphs and rearrange the existing paragraphs. You may also have to rethink your main ideas. You most certainly will have to add transitional sentences and words to link pargraphs.

Here are two modified paragraphs from a term paper written by a high school student. Notice that the connection between the following two paragraphs is not too clear:

As our country was expanding westward, it must have been somewhat difficult distinguishing the good guys from the bad. More than one frontier lawmaker, it seems, spent as much time breaking the law as keeping the peace. The much celebrated Wyatt Earp, for example, supposedly the marshal at Dodge City, was a professional gambler long before he got to Dodge.

He was arrested in Wichita (while a police offi-
cer) for fighting with a man seeking election as
town marshal, and again in Dodge City for
brawling with a dance hall girl.
Bat Masterson was a professional gambler,
owned an interest in the Lone Star Dance Hall
(while wearing a badge), and he, too, was
arrested for rowdyism.

The solution the author of the term paper chose was to add the transitional word *another,* which relates back to the first paragraph, along with a few other words that essentially echo information provided about Wyatt Earp in the first paragraph:

Bat Masterson, **another "superhero" of the**
frontier, *was a professional gambler, owned an*
interest in the Lone Star Dance Hall (while wear-
ing a badge), and he, too, was arrested for row-
dyism.

Such overlapping (the words in boldface) is the key to strong transitions between paragraphs.

A good way to connect paragraphs is to establish a movement of time, like in a narrative, where you tell a story:

First they did this. Later they did that. The fol-
lowing year she went here. Then she went there.
She wound up feeling as if she had never settled
down. That led her back to her family.

In the above example, pretend that each sentence leads off with a new paragraph.

Transition words that connect sentences are also useful in connecting paragraphs: finally, in the meantime, in addition, for example, a telling example is, however, the word instead.

WILL YOU DIVIDE INTO SECTIONS?

If you didn't divide your paper into formal sections in your rough draft, you may want to do so now. Sectioning usually works well in a long paper; in a short paper it may be unnecessary. Sectioning is a good way to organize large chunks of information that may be hard to connect. However, too many sections can also fragment your presentation. Even sections need transitions!

Your outline will suggest divisions in your presentation. You might look it over again.

READ FOR STYLE AND LANGUAGE

Now read the paper with an eye for style and language. Do you have strong transitions between sentences, or are your sentences just slopped down with no thought to how they work together?

Do you have too many big words? Too many small words? What about paragraph and sentence length? Is there some variety, or are all your paragraphs two sentences long and all your sentences six words long? Random lengths will ensure variety: long, short, very long, very long, medium, very short, short, very short, medium, medium, short, long—this sort of pattern (actually a nonpattern) can be your guide.

Make the necessary changes.

CHECK YOUR FACTS

Check your facts. This is something you may overlook. You may assume you got everything right the first time. There is a good chance, however, that even if you took notes accurately, you mangled something when converting your notes into a rough draft.

Ideally you should go through all of your note cards and compare the facts with those in the paper. Since you have been adding, deleting, and rearranging material, too, it is possible that you will make mistakes. Check names and dates, and fix discrepancies. (You may say your subject was born in 1896 in one paragraph and in 1897 in another.) Make sure quotations are accurate and that paraphrases do not resemble a quotation so closely that you are guilty of plagiarism.

CHECK SPELLING
AND GRAMMAR

When in doubt about the spelling of a word, use your dictionary. Not following up on such doubts is probably the cause of half the misspellings people make. Spelling checker programs are available with most popular word processing programs. These will highlight possible spelling errors but will not, unfortunately, correct them for you. A spelling checker cannot tell you, either, whether you meant "led" or "lead."

Look for dangling modifiers ("Looking in the icebox, the ice cream was melting": Was the ice cream looking in the icebox?), run-on sentences ("Gold was discovered in Nevada County and Joe raised horses but Sue didn't know the time of day they lived in a large house and made a lot of money."), and sentence fragments ("They lived in a house. And made a lot of money. From making jewelry."). Have you used words correctly (changed "Its over there" to "It's over there" and "She gave the dog it's bone" to "She gave the dog its bone")? Computer programs cannot fix errors in grammar or punctuation—at least not popular programs.

Computer programs may be able to tell you how many times certain words are used in your paper. You may have the habit of using *thus* in every third sentence. The program will point this out to you. The search-and-replace function common in many word processing programs will allow you to change all your misspellings of Wyat Earp to Wyatt Earp with little more than a couple of keystrokes.

PREPARE
THE "WRAPPER"

The "wrapper" (for want of a better word) is the title page, the table of contents, and the lists of illustrations and tables, if you have them.

Check with your teacher on how he or she wants the title page prepared. Usually all you need is the title, your name, and the section number of your class. Everything is centered.

Depending on the length of the paper, a table of contents may or may not be needed. A good rule of thumb is to include one only if the paper is longer than ten pages. The table of contents should list all the main parts of your paper, including the introduction; chapters or sections; lists of illustrations, tables, graphs, and so forth; and bibliography.

USE ILLUSTRATIONS,
GRAPHS, AND TABLES
ONLY AS NECESSARY

Illustrations (photographs, drawings, diagrams) may be an essential part of your paper on the feeding habits of whales but may be unnecessary in your paper analyzing the fiction of Toni Morrison.

Avoid using illustrations unless you are required to by your teacher, or if you have to have them to illustrate some of your points. Maps may be necessary when you are discussing how quickly tropical rain forests are disappearing. Diagrams may be essential if you are explaining how a house is built. Photographs can be

BAT MASTERSON AND WYATT EARP:

SYMBOLS OF FRONTIER JUSTICE

_____

A Term Paper

Presented to

Mr. Schaeffer

MMI Preparatory School

_____

In Partial Fulfillment

of the Requirements

for Junior American History

_____

by

Matt Stephen Gimmer

April 22, 1985

A sample cover page

useful when you are comparing styles of art, fashion, architecture, or automobiles.

Graphs, charts, and tables can be useful for presenting statistics. Statistics are an excellent way of supporting various types of arguments.

Never cut illustrations out of library materials. Make photocopies instead. If you make your own drawings, use a black pen; avoid colored markers or crayons. Keep the drawings simple. Label the appropriate parts of the drawings in ink or with typed labels.

Title each illustration, table, graph, or chart and place it as close to the corresponding text as possible. You also could number them and place them at the end of the manuscript, with references to them by number in the body of the text. Tables, charts, and graphs may be more effective if used within the text, however. You will have to leave room when you are typing or word-processing, unless you are using software that allows you to create and then merge graphs and tables with the text.

Prepare a list of illustrations or tables, charts, and graphs, but only if you have more than a few of them. Include the title, number of the illustration or table, and page number in the paper for each.

TYPE OR PRINT
THE FINAL DRAFT

Now type or print out the final draft of your term paper.

Leave margins of at least an inch all the way around, and always double-space, except footnotes (unless you are instructed otherwise). Margins of 10–65 are standard; 15–65 leaves room if you plan to put the paper into a folder or punch holes.

If you are using a word processor, you can be fancy and center section titles, justify the text (making all the words along the right-hand margin line up), use italics for emphasis, and so forth. Although the resulting paper will undoubtedly look better than a typed paper, your grade will still be based on the contents of the paper. Use trimmings discreetly and only to make the paper easier to read.

Use white paper only; if you type, use "bond" paper but not erasable, which smears. Type or print on one side of the page only. Use a fresh ribbon in your typewriter or printer.

Number each page in the upper right-hand corner or in the top center. Number each page except the title page and any lists of illustrations or tables you include.

Staple the pages of the paper or place it in a report cover.

A FINAL WORD

Even though term papers are usually required assignments, writing them can bring you many benefits.

You not only learn about a topic you may know little or nothing about, you will also learn important skills in communications: how to find information, how to organize information, and how to convey information in written language.

Think, too, of the term paper as a challenge where you can prove yourself.

And finally, if you adopt a positive attitude toward the assignment, you may even have some fun along the way!

BOOKS FOR
FURTHER READING

Bernstein, Theodore M. *The Careful Writer: A Modern Guide to English Usage.* New York: Atheneum, 1965.

Brady, John. *The Craft of Interviewing.* New York: Random House, 1977.

Carey, Helen H., and Judith E. Greenberg. *How to Use Primary Sources.* New York: Franklin Watts, 1983.

Ellis, Barbara L. *How to Write Themes and Term Papers.* 2nd ed. Woodbury, N.Y.: Barron, 1981.

Flugelman, Andrew, and Jeremy J. Hewes. *Writing in the Computer Age: Word Processing Skills and Style for Every Writer.* New York: Doubleday, 1983.

James, Elizabeth, and Carol Baskin. *How to Write a Term Paper.* New York: Lothrop, Lee, and Shepard, 1980.

Lamm, Kathryn. *10,000 Ideas for Term Papers, Projects, Reports, and Speeches.* 2nd ed. New York: Arco/ Prentice Hall Press, 1987.

McCormick, Mona (ed.) *The New York Times Guide to Reference Materials.* New York: New American Library, 1986.

Mulkerne, Donald J.D., and Donald J.D. Mulkerne, Jr. *The Term Paper: Step by Step.* New York: Anchor Press/Doubleday, 1983.

Provost, Gary. *100 Ways to Improve Your Writing.* New York: New American Library, 1985.

Santa, Beauel M., and Lois L. Hardy. *How to Use the Library.* 2nd ed. Palo Alto, Calif.: Pacific Books, 1966.

Semmelmer, Madeline, and Donald O. Bolander. *Instant English Handbook.* Chicago: Creative Publishing, 1986.

Strunk, William, Jr., and E.B. White. *The Elements of Style.* 3rd ed. New York: Macmillan, 1979.

Turabian, Kate L. *A Manual for Writers of Term Papers, Theses, and Dissertations.* 5th ed. Chicago: University of Chicago Press, 1987.

Venolia, Jan. *Write Right!* Berkeley, Calif.: Ten Speed Press, 1982.

INDEX

ABOUT
THE AUTHOR

Nancy Everhart is an educational media specialist and computer science teacher at MMI Preparatory School in Freeland, Pennsylvania. She is also a consultant, a book reviewer, and a member of the board of directors of the public library in Tamaqua, Pennsylvania, where she makes her home.